The ABC's of Beginning French Language

A Children's Learn French Books

BABY PROFESSOR

EDUCATION KIDS

Speedy Publishing LLC
40 E. Main St. #1156
Newark, DE 19711
www.speedypublishing.com

ANANAS

Ananas   Ananas

BONBON

Bonbon Bonbon

CHIEN

Chien   Chien

DINOSAURE

Dinosaure   Dinosaure

Review Exercise # 1

Match the French word to its corresponding English translation.

Ananas •   • Dog

Bonbon •   • Pineapple

Chien •   • Sweet

Dinosaure •   • Dinosaur

ESCARGOT

Escargot   Escargot

FOURMI

Fourmi   Fourmi

GRENOUILLE

Grenouille   Grenouille

HÉRISSON

Hérisson   Hérisson

Review Exercise # 2

Match the French word to its corresponding English translation.

Escargot •   • Hedgehog

Fourmi •   • Snail

Grenouille •   • Ant

Hērisson •   • Frog

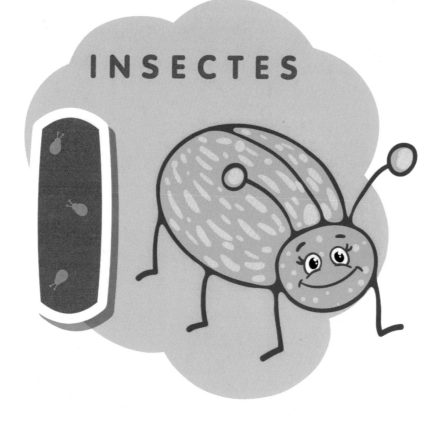

INSECTES

Insectes   Insectes

JOURNAL

Journal   Journal

KARATÉ

Karaté Karaté

LAPIN

Lapin Lapin

Review Exercise # 3

Match the French word to its corresponding English translation.

Insectes •   • Karate

Journal •   • Newspaper

Karatē •   • Insect

Lapin •   • Rabbit

MONSTRE

Monstre   Monstre

NOISETTE

Noisette   Noisette

ORANGE

Orange   Orange

POIVRE

Poivre   Poivre

Review Exercise # 4

Match the French word to its corresponding English translation.

Monstre •   • Orange

Noisette •   • Monster

Orange •   • Hazelnuts

Poivre •   • Pepper

QUILLE

Q

Quille   Quille

ROUE

Roue   Roue

SOURIS

Souris   Souris

TOMATE

Tomate   Tomate

Review Exercise # 5

Match the French word to its corresponding English translation.

Quille •   • Wheel

Roue •   • Skittles

Souris •   • Tomato

Tomate •   • Mouse

UNICORNE

Unicorne   Unicorne

VIOLET

Violet   Violet

WAGON

Wagon   Wagon

Review Exercise # 6

Match the French word to its corresponding English translation.

Unicorne •   • Violet

Violet •   • Rail Car

Wagon •   • Unicorn

XYLOPHONE

Xylophone   Xylophone

YAOURT

Yaourt   Yaourt

ZÉBRE

Zébre   Zébre

Review Exercise # 7

Match the French word to its corresponding English translation.

Xylophone •

• Zebra

Yaourt •

• Xylophone

Zébre •

• Yogurt

Extra Blank Lines

_____

- -

_____

- -

_____

- -

_____

- -

_____

- -

_____

Answers

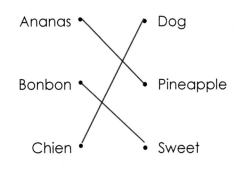

Ananas — Sweet
Bonbon — Sweet
Chien — Dog
Ananas — Pineapple

Dog
Pineapple
Sweet

Dinosaure — Dinosaur

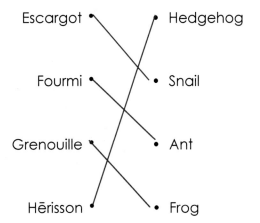

Escargot — Snail
Fourmi — Ant
Grenouille — Frog
Hérisson — Hedgehog

Hedgehog
Snail
Ant
Frog

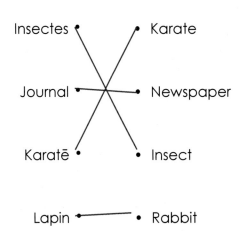

Insectes — Insect
Journal — Newspaper
Karaté — Karate

Karate
Newspaper
Insect

Lapin — Rabbit

Quille •   • Wheel

Roue •   • Skittles

Souris •   • Tomato

Tomate •   • Mouse

Unicorne •   • Violet

Violet •   • Rail Car

Wagon •   • Unicorn

Monstre •   • Orange

Noisette •   • Monster

Orange •   • Hazelnuts

Poivre •   • Pepper

Xylophone •   • Zebra

Yaourt •   • Xylophone

Zébre •   • Yogurt

Visit

BABY PROFESSOR
EDUCATION KIDS

www.BabyProfessorBooks.com

to download Free Baby Professor eBooks
and view our catalog of new and exciting
Children's Books

Made in the USA
Columbia, SC
28 April 2019